101 Reasons Why We Should Leave the EU

Formal notes, contact det

101 Reasons Why We Should Leave the EU.

eBook edition January 2019. ISBN 978-1-90965(

First published in 2011 by St Edward's Press Ltd, Company Number: 04035239.

For hard copies of this booklet, or further information, please contact St Edward's Press Ltd – See contact details below. Single hard copy: £4 each including UK postage. Generous discounts available for multiple hard copies. Payment may be made by PayPal for website orders, or credit/debit card, on-line payments, cheques etc., for other orders

Contact details:
Registered Office and orders by post
20 Barra Close, Highworth, Swindon, Wilts, SN6 7HX

Phone: 01793 762417 (This business is run from home and so the phone may not always be answered. Call 01752 334950 if you want to leave a message during office hours.)

Email: info@stedwardspress.co.uk   Website: www.stedwardspress.co.uk

While every effort has been made to ensure that this publication by St Edward's Press Ltd provides accurate information, neither the publisher, author, retailer nor any other supplier shall be liable to any person or entity with respect to any loss or damage caused by, or alleged to be caused by, the information contained in, or omitted from, this publication.

101 Reasons Why We Should Leave The EU

By Hugh Williams

101 Reasons Why We Should Leave The EU.

By Hugh Williams

Introduction

This eBook edition of *101 Reasons why we should leave the EU* has been prepared in the early part of January 2019 in response to the parliamentary stalemate with which 2018 drew to a close.

This stalemate arose because the British electorate voted to leave the EU in 2016, whereas the majority of the British Members of Parliament were in favour of the country remaining a member. With the British establishment (The Government, the Churches, Parliament, the Banks, Industry, the Arts, Broadcasting and most of the Press) having long been in favour of our membership of the EU, but the British public feeling quite otherwise, as 2019 begins, the country faces what many believe to be its worst constitutional crisis since the so-called "Glorious Revolution."

With the country thus polarised, and with many voters still not sure of the underlying reasons for leaving the EU, this eBook version of a booklet, which made a not-inconsiderable contribution to the 2016 Referendum campaign (Sales of it thus far exceed 40,000), has been published to provide a list of some of those reasons.

Returning democracy to Westminster

1.   I would like to start this list with my own personal reason for voting to leave the EU, although it is a reason shared by many millions of others. I voted to leave because I wanted to restore British democracy to our Westminster Parliament. That was the only reason I made that decision. I did not vote to leave because of the oft - considered issue of immigration, or the costs of our membership, or for any other reason than my wish to see this country run its own affairs as it did before it joined the then Common Market in 1973. What the referendum vote has decided is to implement this very decision and, once it has been effected, then we, as a nation, through our national parliament, will, once again, be the ones who decide what changes to make to our own laws, including issues like immigration. Such matters will no longer be decided for us but by unelected bureaucrats working overseas.

Having started with this fundamentally important reason let's now look at a further 100 reasons in favour of our departure from the EU…

Let's start by looking at those areas that the EU controls:

2.   Although, in June 2016, the people of Britain were given a referendum on our
membership of the European Union, for over forty years before that, the British
people were never asked if they wanted to be part of a European Union. There had
been a referendum in 1975 but that simply asked voters if they wanted to remain in the
Common Market. The actual wording was "Do you think the United Kingdom should
stay in the European Community (The Common Market)?" However, since 1975 the
Common Market has grown into something far more significant than a mere trading
club as we have seen power after power removed from these shores to be exercised by
Brussels. Of itself this extraordinary loss of power should have been addressed by
Parliament but whenever anyone questioned this state of affairs, they were labelled
with descriptions like nut-cases or right-wing extremists.
What these people were complaining about, amongst other matters, was the fact that
the EU controls the following areas that they wished to see returned to Westminster:

3. Foreign affairs	4. Economic affairs	5. Public Health
6. Justice	7. Energy	8. Employment
9. Police	10. Environment	11. Immigration
12. Social Affairs	13. Farming	14. Fisheries
15. Law Enforcement	16. Transport	

In short, the decision of the referendum on June 23rd, 2016 was to make sure that this
abrogation of power by our elected representatives stopped and that it should never
happen again. Of course, it might be argued that, perhaps, the EU is indeed the best
place for these matters to be decided, and not in Westminster, but that is an argument
that can never be sustained when one looks at…

The EU's lack of Democracy:
17.   The EU is a totally undemocratic institution. The rules are made by unelected
bureaucrats in the European Commission; they write the laws, decide the agenda and
timing of their consideration, and then get them passed by the almost entirely pro-EU
European Parliament – a parliament that has no official opposition. The EU
Commission controls the funding and enforcement of laws on the member states.
There is no way for an elected MEP to force repeal of legislation.
18.   The whole plan is for the EU to do away with all the member countries and
form just one country, Europe. This would mean that …

19.   The parliaments of the EU member states will be neutered as Brussels takes total charge.

20.   As already noted, when we voted in the 1975 Referendum, we were told we were joining a trading agreement. Now that the official government documents, concerning our entry in 1973, have been released (such as FCO 30/1048) we have seen that our then Conservative Government had it clearly in mind that we were on a long road to full political union, but ministers were told not to tell the British people. This means that this ever-creeping European Union (the gradual and now almost complete takeover of twenty-eight European countries by the EU) has all been done with the full connivance of the British Conservative and Labour Parties and the wholehearted enthusiasm of the Lib Dems.

21.   Although we have now had the 2016 referendum, before that vote, while we had been promised chances to leave the EU, all of the promises were broken. Firstly, Tony Blair promised us a referendum on the EU constitution in the 2005 General Election manifesto. When this constitution (national straitjacket) went through our Westminster Parliament under the name of the Treaty of Lisbon, that promise was broken, with the total support of the Liberal Democrats.

Secondly, the Conservatives, who were then the official opposition, gave us a cast-iron guarantee that we would be given a referendum on this treaty, but within a few months of being elected, they too had broken their promise over this matter of vital national interest again with the connivance of the Liberal Democrats.

It has only been thanks to the growing tide of opposition to the EU dictatorship within Britain that David Cameron was forced to seek some changes on the terms of our membership on which we were then asked to vote in June 2016.

David Cameron thought that what he had been promised by the Brussels Bureaucrats would be enough to swing the vote in favour of "Remain", but the electorate could easily see through the hopeless inadequacy of the concessions that he had been given and so, and very sensibly, voted to leave.

All of this shows that the result of the vote in June 2016 was a powerful, yet all-too fragile lifeline towards regaining our national independence and, with so many powers-that-be determined to stop that happening, especially in the EU, it is vital that we keep fighting to ensure that democracy wins the day over dictatorship, especially at this time of national crisis.

22.   MEPs cannot initiate legislation. Only the unelected European Commission can do that. There is very little point in having Members of the European Parliament (MEPs). The European Parliament is a sham; indeed it must be when very few people can name the MEPs who represent their region.

23.   Because of the way that EU voting works, even if UK MEPs (of all parties) voted as a single block, they have insufficient numbers to block legislation that is harmful to British interests.

24.   MEPs are asked to vote on hundreds of items in an hour. This means that they can get confused as to which measure they are voting for. The MEPs nearly always vote in favour of a version of the Commission's proposal because, as has just been said, most MEPs are pro-EU. Indeed the voting system in the European Parliament is so skewed that legislation is nearly always passed. This has always been the case. If a piece of legislation fails, then it comes back again and again until it is passed.

25.   There is seldom a proper vote count in the European Council. There isn't even a _wish_ to have a proper vote count.

26.   Criticism of the EU is definitely not encouraged in the European Parliament. (See also Reasons 95 to 97.)

27.   The British gave democracy to the World. Yet, unless we can properly leave the EU, we will have abandoned this system (which has proved its integrity over eight centuries) in favour of a very anti-democratic dictatorship.

28.   Acquis Communautaire. This is the Brussels Ratchet which has the effect that, once a national power has been ceded to Brussels, it will never be returned. Indeed this Acquis is just what the Eurocrats want because...

29.   "Ever closer union" is what the EU is all about (It is stressed right at the start of the Lisbon Treaty) and "Ever closer union" is what it has always been about; but, of course, not with the approval of the peoples of Europe. As with all EU legislation, this union is being foisted on the member states by the unelected Brussels bureaucrats. And indeed, its imposition was shown to be totally contrary to the wishes of people like the Irish, Dutch and French voters, all of whom voted _against_ the EU constitution, (which within a short term had morphed into the Treaty of Lisbon) in three of the rare referendums that were actually granted to EU voters on the subject.

30.   The three main political parties refuse to deal honestly with the issue of the EU. They always focus on national (internal) issues, and _never on the far more important issue of who actually governs us_. Our MPs are frightened to let you know just how much the EU bosses them about.

31.   With the EU making so many of our laws, there is little point worrying about the national policies of any of the British political parties. This is because, when in government, they _have_ to dance to the EU's tune, not to the one they present in their manifesto. Once we can return our seat of government to Westminster and replace EU Law with UK law, only then it will make sense to have a full presentation and debate about the different manifestos.

32.   Two fundamental principles have been destroyed by our EU membership:

a.   The hard-won right to elect <u>and dismiss</u> those who propose our laws. The Brussels Bureaucrats who do so are unelected.

And

b.   We have given our UK Parliament, and only that Parliament, the right to make our laws. But this right has been given by our UK Parliament to a foreign power, without our permission, and all the while the three main political parties pretend that they have not done this.

33.   We, in Britain, are simply powerless to change any EU law. With 13% share in the Council of Ministers the maths simply does not work in favour of national interests and wishes because you need 30% to block new EU laws. This is called Qualified Majority Voting (QMV).

With our own MPs in Westminster powerless to change, or prevent, EU law being enacted, all we can do is the bidding of our EU dictators. And…

34.   …If we don't put EU law into effect, we face huge fines from Brussels.

35.   No law passed in Brussels has ever been successfully overturned by the UK Parliament. For example...

36.   The British Government can no longer ban live animal exports. It does not take too much imagination to visualise the suffering caused to these dumb creatures on the journeys which usually last for thousands of miles across Europe. But Westminster can do nothing about it.

37.   The only appeal is to the European Court of Justice (which meets in Luxembourg), but no appeal will ever work because <u>the Court must always find in favour of "ever-closer union"</u>. Democracy is not what the EU is about...

38.   As if to prove this, a junior government minister was heard to say in early October 2010. "I am coming round to the Eurosceptic point of view about the EU. Whenever I go to Brussels to negotiate the British position, I am allowed three minutes to make a prepared statement, as are all the other 27 ministers. None of it makes a blind bit of difference. What is decided is what the Commission has already decreed long before the national ministers turn up. There is no debate. No negotiation. It's all a stitch-up". So there we have it from the horse's mouth.

Here are just some of the over one hundred thousand rules that the EU has imposed upon us

39.   European Arrest Warrant. This means that you can be extradited to another EU state, without charge and sometimes merely for questioning. It is done at the whim of a foreign judge and our legal system is powerless to do anything to prevent it. And this is no mere threat; it has already happened to hundreds of UK citizens, with

precious little reporting about it in the Press. This growing list of extreme injustices proves just how totally unjust this EU law is; and it's an EU law to which the Labour Government, that was in power between 1997 and 2010, signed us up; and are proud of having done so.

40.   Prisoners getting the right to vote.

41.   Money Laundering Regulations. All that palaver when we want to change our bank account or appoint a new accountant. It all comes from the EU.

42.   Inefficient Light Bulbs. These so-called eco-friendly bulbs that are so dim when switched on and never last for as long as we are told they will. In addition, they contain so much mercury that, if you break one, you should vacate the room immediately and leave all the windows open for fifteen minutes while the deadly poisonous vapour disperses. All thanks to the EU.

43.   Thousands of Post Office Closures. Again thanks to the EU's regulations.

44.   Rubbish Collection. The new way we have to leave out our rubbish is an EU imposition with heavy fines for our councils if we don't obey their laws. And there are even rumours that some of what we sort so diligently for recycling never even gets recycled but gets dumped in the sea.

45.   Value Added Tax has replaced the UK's Purchase Tax. VAT is an EU tax, a portion of which is paid to the EU.

46.   Political Correctness. All of this (never daring to, for example, "call a spade a spade", or using phrases like "nitty gritty") is part and parcel of the EU's dominating culture.

Let's look at some further effects of the EU's dictatorial regime

47.   While bandying statistics can be risky, even EU officials have declared that over 70% of our national laws already come from Brussels.

48.   Brussels issues, on average, nine new laws or regulations every day.

49.   The Common Agricultural Policy gobbles up £65billion of our money, yet farm incomes continue to fall. We are told that this money helps our farmers. Poppycock! It is actually paid to our farms whether they produce anything or not! In addition, the farming community is now under such stress that, on average, one farmer commits suicide each week.

50.   New Zealand butter, which is virtually subsidy-free and, after being shipped half-way around the world, is cheaper on our supermarket shelves than EU brands. The Common Agricultural Policy really stinks, doesn't it?

51.   Certain areas in the UK, for example the South West of Britain, are no longer meant to be used for farming. Brussels has designated it (the whole region) for

tourism. There is a map in Brussels where this is clearly set out. Farmers in Devon are not meant to be farming.

Costs of membership

52.   It costs us about £54 million every working day (an average of £14 billion every year between 2013/14 to 2019/20) just to belong. (Figures were provided by H M Treasury in January 2015.)

53.   It is reckoned to cost a further £220 million every day (£80 billion a year) to simply comply with EU regulations.

54.   Much of the EU funding that we receive must be "match-funded" by our government.

55.   What we spend on our membership of the EU could be better spent on schools, hospitals and the police. That's the equivalent of £250 that you, personally, and I are paying every year simply to belong to this club that we never voted for. It's enough for 50 brand-new fully-equipped 800 bed hospitals every year.

56.   And remember, the money the EU doles out to us is not them being generous. It was our money in the first place.

57.   When the EU provides funding for a UK project, they are simply giving some of our own money back on the basis that we will spend it as they wish, and often requiring us to add further money for the same purpose.

Regionalisation

58.   The EU wants to run this country by means of twelve regional authorities, all reporting direct to Brussels.

59.   As one region in 250 throughout Europe, do you think that, for example, the people living in the South West of England - the Euro region known as UK "K" - will ever be listened to?

60.   The county of Devon (as well as those of Cornwall and the rest of them) is set to disappear as the regions take over.

61.   All this talk of regional assemblies by both the Press as well as the present government is a smokescreen for *European* regional assemblies. We are told that we, the British people, want regions. This is poppycock again! "Poppycock" because we have simply never been asked! The EU is determined to dominate and emasculate our national government, by dividing up the member countries through this creeping regionalisation.

62.   If you doubt my word that this is happening, next time you visit cities like Exeter, look at the sign as you drive in. No longer is Exeter the Cathedral City of

Devon, it is now the European *Regional Capital*. This European regional institution is costing local taxpayers £5million a year to run.

The end of the nation state

63.   If we are not able to leave the EU and we let regionalisation develop as the EU wants, England will not have the consolation of still being the name of a region. England will disappear and be split up into the outlines we can already see clearly drawn on the Brussels map and in which we vote in the elections for the EU Parliament. Do you want England to disappear – without your even being consulted? Indeed...

64.   The map of Europe in Brussels no longer mentions England as a country.

65.   You may think that Scotland and Wales are countries but, according to the EU, they are simply regions.

66.   One possible result of the current Brexit negotiations, if M Michel Barnier has his way over the border between Northern Ireland and the Republic of Ireland, might be the break-up of the UK.

67.   The EU wants to do away with all EU monarchies.

68.   The EU wants to abolish all national identities, even suggesting that, for example, the South of England should be merged with the North of France to form a new super region called the Trans Manche region.

The threat to our financial independence

69.   For many years the EU has been trying to take control of the UK's financial centre, the City of London. The City of London (the largest financial centre in the world) provides over 12% of our GDP, £52 billion of tax, and 1.1 million jobs in this country. The City has played an incredibly important part of our economy, and its performance is capable of turning a negative balance of trade into a positive balance of payments. Without the City of London our nation's finances would be sunk.

70.   On top of this, the EU seeks to impose a Financial Transaction Tax, with extra-territorial effect, which will make the EU even more uncompetitive in a global market. 800 years ago, Magna Carta enshrined the principle of "No taxation without representation" – the EU has simply done away with that concept. We pay taxes to the EU but have no say in how the money is spent.

Corruption in the EU

71.   The EU is riddled with corruption. In 1998 every single EU Commissioner had to resign because of endemic EU corruption. There is a culture of systemic greed and denial of any sense of responsibility on the Brussels gravy train.

72.	The European Union's finances are corrupt. Its accounts have contained significant errors for the past twenty-three years (1994 to 2017). What this means is that the EU's expenditure is not properly controlled. If you or I did such a thing we would fall foul of the EU's Money Laundering Regulations and be put in prison. But not our European dictators; they simply get clean away with this corruption and scandal. But it's worse than this…

73.	Anyone who works at a position of responsibility in the European Union enjoys a life-time's immunity from prosecution. So they can never be punished for these crimes. We are told that European law protects its citizens. Well, it does. It protects criminals from ever being punished, just so long as they are committing crimes in the name of the EU.

74.	And to prove this, in May 2004 the European Parliament voted not to punish those guilty of European corruption.

75.	In 1997 I asked (the now late) Sir Leon Brittan if it were true that, at that time, our gold and currency reserves were being transferred to the European Central Bank in Frankfurt. He said that they were. Don't you think we should have been told?

76.	The EU is fundamentally anti-Christian. The EU's School Diary for 2011 marked all the religious festivals for Hindus, Sikhs, Mohammedans, Jews, and Chinese BUT NOT FOR Christians. Neither Christmas nor Easter was mentioned. When objections were raised, the EU officials responsible replied by saying they would solve this problem by ensuring that the next year's diary had no religious festivals marked at all! Added to this, Baroness Ashton, the (then) EU's High Representative for Foreign Affairs, announced in February 2011 that it is no longer politically correct to use the word "Christian". It should also be noted that the move to legalise gay marriage emanated from the EU.

The Treaty of Lisbon (the EU's constitution)

77.	The Treaty of Lisbon has one very worrying aspect to it. It is self-amending which means the EU can now do whatever it wants. No further treaties (sic) will ever need to be passed by national referendums again.

78.	Having accepted the new Constitution, unless we do eventually leave, we are effectively locked in forever. Do you feel happy that you, your children, grandchildren, successors etc., are now bound to such a prospect?

The Euro

79.	Having ratified the Treaty of Lisbon, and despite the reassurances given by both Chancellor of the Exchequer, George Osborne, and David Cameron, that we will never give up the pound, thanks to a measure passed overwhelmingly by our MPs in

March 2011, if we are unable to leave the EU, we would be in grave danger of losing the pound and adopting the Euro. This was because the Treaty of Lisbon says that the currency of the EU shall be the Euro; so *using the Euro is now a condition of EU membership*. If we are able unable to leave the EU, it is unlikely we will be able to remain outside the Euro for much longer.

80.   Once locked into the Euro there would be no escape. The pound will have gone forever.

The Advantages of leaving the EU

81.   Once out of the EU, we will naturally sign a trade deal with the EU, just like over 70 other countries have already done. Yes, there may be current difficulties in reaching an agreement with the EU as to what that deal might look like, but, with so many other countries having signed one, and with EU companies very keen to keep selling is their goods, there can be little doubt that an agreement will be signed (as to what that might look like, please refer to our sister publication *Brexit Choices*, available on the St Edward's Press website.) And if the EU fails to be economically sensible and co-operative over the Brexit negotiations, then it just proves that we were right to vote to leave such an organisation that has so little regard for the economic well-being of its citizens and neighbours.

82.   Once outside, we can benefit our loyal Commonwealth friends by, once again, being able to buy more from them and at terms we negotiate with them directly.

83.   Once out, unemployment will not increase materially. The simple reason why this is so is that we buy so much from the EU, if they refuse to buy our goods, we would simply retaliate by refusing to buy theirs. And this would really hurt them far more than us, since we buy far more from them than they buy from us. Please do not be fooled into thinking that we would suffer, once we are out. It should be noted that, having voted for Brexit, the UK is enjoying a forty year low in unemployment.

84.   The two European countries that are not part of the EU, Norway and Switzerland, are among the richest on the Continent. So, again, here is a clear indication that we will not suffer when we leave. Even Neil Kinnock has stated that, if we were to come out of the EU, we would suffer no trade tariffs.

85.   Once out of the EU we could change the practice of having to mark our goods with labels of dubious worth, such as the one reading "This Salmon may contain fish".

86.   It is a little-known fact that the citizens of Switzerland (not an EU country) export four times as much per head of population to the EU as do the citizens of the UK. This shows that one does not need to be in the EU to export successfully to the EU.

The EU has all of the attributes of a country in its own right – such as its own flag, anthem, territory, citizenship, judiciary etc.

87.	France has called for the EU to set up its own army and recently the President of the European Commission, Jean-Claude Juncker has called for the same. If you doubt that the new constitution heralds the arrival of a single country called Europe, does not the existence of an EU army imply that that single country called the EU has already been born? ...

88.	As does the arrival of a European President and also...

89.	The EU now has an unelected European Foreign Minister called the High Representative for Foreign Affairs. This person has a large salary of over £300,000 and the department, the EU's Foreign Service (the EU External Action Service voted for by the Conservative Government, please note) has the following: a £6 billion budget; a workforce of 7,000; a network of 137 embassies; 46 diplomats in the Caribbean; a head office costing £10.5 million with a £32 million fleet of bullet-proof limousines. None of which is needed because this service simply duplicates what is already being done by the member states. (The plan is so clearly a key part of doing away with and replacing the member states.) Not only was this EU Foreign Service voted for by Conservative MEPs; the Conservative Party rubbed salt in the nation's wounds by selling their former headquarters in Smith Square in London to the EU so that the new EU embassy in London could be based there.

90.	The European Central Bank – the existence of which is another clear sign that the EU regards itself as a country.

EU waste and destruction

91.	There are so many members of the EU now that the costs of translating the proceedings of the institutions has escalated exponentially from £200 million when there were 15 members to close to £1billion per year.

92.	The EU has two parliament buildings. One in Brussels and the other in Strasbourg, which is used just 48 days a year. It costs more than £100 million a year to shuttle everything between the two. What a waste of time and money!

93.	Yet the European Library is in another place, Luxembourg. It costs £50,000 per book lent. What a waste of money. What madness!

94.	The European Fisheries policy results in more perfectly edible fish being thrown back into the sea than are actually landed. Yet this same policy has imposed ever-diminishing quotas to try to restore the depleted fishing stocks this policy is itself creating, throwing thousands of UK fishermen out of work. 9,000 jobs have been lost in the fishing industry since we joined the Common Market in 1973. Indeed, this same policy – this severe depletion of our fish stocks – is resulting in EU fishermen moving into African waters and, as has happened in UK fishing waters, forcing the locals out of their own fishing waters and costing them their livelihoods.

Nobody is allowed to criticise the EU

95.   Anyone in Brussels who speaks out against what is going on (like Nigel Farage MEP, former MEPs Marta Andreasen and Godfrey Bloom, or Martin Tillack) is punished. They are punished for telling us what is really going on. (See more about Marta Andreasen under Reason no 101.)

96.   We are told that, in future, the EU will fund pro-EU election propaganda in the member states.

97.   Criticism of the EU is considered to be blasphemous. The Advocate General of the European Court of Justice gave it as his formal opinion in case C274/99P that "Criticism of the EU is akin to blasphemy and could be restricted without violating freedom of speech".

How the Labour and Conservative Parties, as well as the Media, used to do all they could to help the EU

98.   No cost-benefit analysis. One would have thought that with all these problems in the EU, with its deep unpopularity in this country; with, until 2016, the people never having been asked if they want to belong to it; with it costing so much just to be a member and with no discernible benefits to be gained from this topsy-turvy arrangement whereby we pay them vast sums for the privilege of being dictated to by them; one would have thought that it would have been sensible for the Government to have carried out a cost-benefit analysis of our membership of the EU. But, no. All they used to say was that it was in our nation's interest to belong to the EU without saying why. Indeed, it was their "Nanny knows best" attitude that was partly responsible for the voters deciding to vote as they did in the 2016 referendum.

99.   Secrecy (Conspiracy?) in the Press and the media. For years, the Press and the media (as well as politicians of the three main parties) have belittled and ridiculed those of us who have tried to protest about the way we hand £54 million per day for the "privilege" of being dictated to. Being sneered at, and on the receiving end of both opprobrium and name-calling have been the lot of the Eurosceptics. Why should that be, unless the Press and the media are part of this same anti-democratic, anti-Christian EU stream roller?

UKIP has been the main recipient of this besmirching with the BBC always and deliberately describing UKIP as "far right." But why? UKIP is the most cosmopolitan and democracy-loving party there is. All UKIP wants is for our seat of government to be returned to Westminster, where we can vote in our MPs and then get rid of them at the next election if we don't like what they have done. What is remotely right-wing about that?

Of course one must not overlook the Daily Express campaign that started in December 2010 calling for the UK to leave the EU and, very recently, other papers joining their bandwagon, not to mention a number of MPs and former MPs having openly campaigned to leave the EU. But why has there been this past mistreatment of the Eurosceptic movement as if they (we) are all part of the great unwashed (and worse)?

This was the scene in 2009, when I was working with a lady to try to get some publicity for Marta Andreasen's jaw-dropping exposé of the EU in her book "Brussels Laid Bare". This PR lady tried so hard to promote Marta's book to the Press, but this is what she found. She said:

"I was extremely surprised when I tried to promote Marta's book to the media. There were journalists whom I know quite well and who returned my phone calls with warmth and good will, but the minute I mentioned 'UKIP', they went catatonic and clammed up.

"With general calls, some individuals were sympathetic, but others were almost openly hostile. There seems to be this perception with many that UKIP are part of the 'extreme right', and therefore not to be touched with a barge-pole.

"I guess part of this will be a top-down reaction - who knows what is said by senior editors and managers to their news teams behind closed doors? I certainly think there were signs that both the media and the main political parties were trying to smother UKIP and starve it of political oxygen in the run-up to the (2009) election."

There can be only one explanation – that the Press have been, and in many cases still are, on the side of the EU.

100.   Brussels Broadcasting Corporation. The BBC receives enormous subsidies and loans from Brussels, with the quid pro quo that they will not criticise the EU. This is public knowledge and it was confirmed by one of the BBC's employees in 2011 when, having been offered some publicity about UKIP, she simply replied "Don't waste time with me. I work for the Brussels Broadcasting Service." Why would a BBC employee say that, unless it were true?

And one last mention of EU corruption to end on…

101.   I have already mentioned Marta Andreasen's book and it would be no bad thing to give a brief résumé of her story as the last point in this catalogue of EU horrors.

Marta was appointed as the EU's Chief Accountant in early 2002. *She was the first professional accountant ever to be appointed to this top financial role in the EU –* which, when you come to think about it, is a dead give-away about the lax way in which the EU runs its finances.

One of her first tasks was to sign off the 2001 accounts that had been prepared by her predecessor. She realised she had better understand them before signing them off and, on inspection, she discovered a €200 million fraud. So she refused to sign the accounts.

You would expect such a discovery and report to result in thanks and gratitude by the powers-that-be in Brussels, but you would be mistaken. Instead of being praised, and rewarded, she was suspended for two years, during which time they investigated to see if she was correct.

After two years, they found that she had indeed been correct but, instead of being reinstated, she was summarily sacked - for disloyalty to the EU.

She appealed against her sacking on the basis of wrongful dismissal. The hearing was in November 2006 and she was told that she would be given the decision in the spring of 2007, but it was not until November 2007 that she was told that she had failed. Please just stop and consider that <u>she had to suffer a delay of 12 months before learning the decision of the hearing</u>. The cruelty that delay involved just shows how the EU treats people who speak the truth about what is really going on in Brussels. After that she took her case to a higher court in 2010 but, you guessed it, she was turned down again. Clearly the EU does not believe in the truth. You can read of her jaw-dropping experiences in her book *Brussels Laid Bare*, published by St Edward's Press (Please see front of book for website and other contact details.)

<u>Clearly, we were very wise to vote to leave the corrupt, dictatorial and totally undemocratic EU and we must ensure that this is indeed what happens.</u>